FIELD TRUST PROJECT

200 Epigrams/Poems of Relationship Mystical and Otherwise

PAMELA CHURCH

To us all everywhere blessings and kindness

Copyright © 2022 Pamela Church

All rights reserved. www.heartbraintrust.com

First paperback edition March 2022
Revised edition June 2024

Book and cover design by David Provolo

Cover art: Abstract Rainbows Catherine Falls Commercial

ISBN 978-0-9795101-1-3 (paperback)
ISBN 978-0-9795101-2-0 (ebook)
Library of Congress Control Number: 2022905047

200 Epigrams/Poems, A Poem, and A Summary: A Long Poem

First Love 10
Place Holder For Emptiness 11
Joining Power And Love 12
Love Dog 13
Quickening And Good Tidings 14
Getting My Red Shoes On 15
Iridescence In The Field 16
You And Me 17
A Broad Wing Span 18
Not Fixed 19
Emergency Flashlight 20
Rainbow Flag 21
Letting It Go 22
Changing It Up 23
Requirements To Meet You 24
Compassion Plus One Makes A Full Circle 25
Mercy Me 26
Air Awareness 27
The Goddess Watches Over 28
Flow And Flux 29
Blessings 30
The Fourth Turning 31
Character Structure 32
Present In My Heart 33
Prism 34
Meiji Shrine 35

Bring Your Bathing Suit Or Not Just Come Swimming 36
Practices For The Time 37
"Magic Is In The Air" 38
Humor From The Void 39
Cooked 40
A Jerk Sometimes 41
I Am Here 42
Holy Work 43
The Distance Of Love 44
L'Amour 45
The Antidote To Ego Investment 46
Speed Of Cherry Petals Falling Down 47
The Fool And The Dog Walking Down The Road 48
A Different Part Of The Brain 49
My Heart Is Met 50
Gritty Today 51
My Dance Teacher 52
Go Figure 53
Headline From Newspaper Stand On The Corner 54
Aspirations 55
Blue Sky Everywhere 56
This Culture 57
Careful 58
What There Is To Work With 59
Competition 60
Boogie Man 61
Flying Colors 62
All Right It Is All Right 63
Gold Watch 64

No Glamorizing Here. 65
Baraqah 66
Ode To The Fool. 67
It Routinely Annoys Me 68
Synapse Between Self And God 69
Singing Me Home. 70
My Hardship Is Polished 71
Taking It Down. 72
Sweet Nothings 73
The Gesture That Calls It. 74
A Nod 75
Thich Nhat Hanh 76
Hanuman 77
The Speed Of Our Time. 78
A Call 79
No Grace Here 80
Remake The World 81
Such A Simple Statement 82
A Mystic Rant 83
This Too. 84
Job Description For A Shaman 85
Collecting 86
Unbounded 87
Where To Go For A Night Swim 88
Sugar 89
You And Me Both 90
A Line Of Light. 91
Following The Arc Of The Land 92
All Of One Piece 93

Reckoning	94
Grace Takes Over	95
Darling I Am Here	96
Wheelhouse Of Time	97
Lonely	98
The Wicked Witch Is Dead	99
Spirit Time	100
The Work Of Coming Home	101
Receiving	102
What Does Shame Have To Do With It	103
Presence Is A Good Thing	104
Tipping The Scales	105
Lushness	106
Use What You Have	107
Initiatory Fees	108
In The Mix	109
Mending The Time	110
Using Everything In Order To Write	111
Less Of Me	112
Know Your Deep Goodness	113
Openness Being Known	114
Over The Moon	115
Mystical Relational Core	116
The Sacred Void And Dream Dance	117
Say What	118
No New News	119
Back Heart	120
The Veil Is Thin Today	121
Dropping Prayers	122
Beginner's Mind	123

A Completion Of The Circle With These Four	124
Prayers Heard Around The World	125
Open Floor Practice	126
Affection Love Gratitude	127
People Do Fly	128
The Lineage Of Devotion	129
Blue Hills	130
Movement Of Mind	131
The Chevron	132
Flood Plains	133
Try It Out	134
Dedicating Merit	135
It Is All There	136
Home Ground	137
For Somebody Else	138
Best Friend	139
My Heart Is Available	140
Swap Meet	141
Pivot Point	142
Dreamtime And The Path With Heart	143
Smooth Sneakers	144
A Directive To My DNA	145
Mystic Warrior	146
Sumptuous Joy Now And Then	147
Nervous System As The Double	148
Mystic Lover Of The World	149
Somewhere Over The Rainbow	150
Sureness Of An Arrow	151
Arrow Through The Void	152
Casting Lines To The Future	153

Body Breathing Moves With Time	154
What We Have Come To	155
Riffing	156
Shaping The Day	157
Tiny Stings And Misunderstandings	158
Being A Prayer Wheel In The World	159
Way Complicated	160
Heart Presence	161
Eyes At The Horizon	162
Once Again	163
Jai Ma	164
Writing Code For My Spirit	165
Field Relationship	166
Down Come The Walls	167
Noticing What Comes From Mind	168
Mystic Time	169
Mind	170
Bless Your Heart	171
Tundra Swans Flying	172
Mindstream	173
Daily Practice	174
Spirit Talent	175
Hey	176
Remembering To Remember	177
Washed Through With Light	178
Relational Field	179
Pilgrim Heart Devotion	180
Dharma Warrior	181
Changing Paradigms	182
Shirofugen Cherry As Taoist Elder	183

Metadata	184
Decency And Hard Times	185
Faceted Jewels Everyone Of Us	186
Routine And Revelation	187
Lay It Down	188
The Edge Of The World	189
Weave Of Wholeness	190
Riff Raff	191
Lines Of Memory	192
Seed Intents	193
I Walk Gratitude	194
A Means To Keep Close	195
The Sun And The Moon	196
The Light Walking On Grey Mornings	197
Fractured You Bet	198
The World Lit From Within	199
"Harmonize Darling"	200
The Goodness That Is You	201
The Mystical Field	202
The Ministry That Calls To Us Each	203
A Thing Of Beauty	204
Train The Heart Like A Warrior	205
Like A Wave	206
Whole Cloth	207
Immersed In Clear Light	208
The Refrain	209
Rilke's Praise	210
A Summary: A Long Poem	211

First Love

The love that carries me
my love for the planet.
Not an abstraction
this deepest part of me.
Receiving this relationship
being this relationship
the world makes sense.
We meet and carry on.
We don't miss a day.

Place Holder For Emptiness

There is a piece of jewelry
I wear everyday
that has a stone missing.
Space touching metal.
Sometimes space touches
my heart and
I remember how to fly.

Joining Power and Love

Power needs love.
Love needs continuance.
Here we are working
both sides of the divide.
Some of us choose one
or the other
rather than saying
"Life is crazy if I drop either one."
Let's name power for what it really is:
vision creativity lots of work.
Illuminate it with love
and the walls come down.

Love Dog

Isn't it what you have always wanted
to be a love dog?
Me too.
My version is in fact my dog.
She is an 12 year old black lab
rescue mutt
who loves to walk
and see the world.
It is crazy how routinely a person,
a child, whomever will say to me
after looking at her
"What a nice dog!"
I didn't understand until I saw another
dog who looks just like my dog.
I got it. My dog, Mia, routinely smiles
as she is exploring the world.
This other dog was doing
the same thing.

Quickening and Good Tidings

don't always go together.
Tenacious patterns that are
only patterns can interfere.
Right now it seems
the planet is shouting it out:
over with these acted out
places of doom.
We have been delirious.
We have been undone.
We forgot that we are
both the light and the ground.
Time to remember.

Getting My Red Shoes On

If I am talking about body
and heart and the world,
I also have to talk about terror.
It is with me like
an old familiar coat.
It can be electric in the body.
It has accompanied me my days
and my nights.
I know the old tropes about
releasing and purifying.
Sure I do that dance.
It works, dance works.
There is a musical piece
I listen to called "Shiva's Dancehall."
That's it. Meet you on the dance floor.

Iridescence In The Field

Always.
But what does it mean?
It means the field is held in light.
Let us go be held,
let the revolution of
loving kindness happen,
let us be held in love light
of the divine,
let us wonder
what we were waiting for.

You And Me

Know I am greedy
for your presence.
I jump into your arms and birds fly
out of my skull.
They are happy
to be a part of
this holy commotion.

A Broad Wing Span

Mystic lover of the world is about me doing my work, you doing your work, all healing the best we can, and meeting up listening to the night sky. This is claiming the need to be vast conscious mindful. Field blessing knowing beloved as sky and earth. The stars concur. We find our wholeness and something else.

Not Fixed

You bet. A definition of dreamtime:
fluid, open, connected, shaman's time.
I don't know if dreamtime can be seen;
I know it can be felt as soft flow and
the presence of the ground holding us.
Eyes open or closed we see more. It
is all about a potential for boundless
compassion and perceiving.

Emergency Flashlight

Have you seen those flashlights that have a crank to them and to get any light, a person has to crank and keep cranking until light momentarily appears? That is a good image of how it works for me. I do my work everyday and glimmers of light come through. I need more light. Do they make hand crank flood lights?

Rainbow Flag

In Peru, in Cusco particularly, rainbow flags fly high. The Incan culture is brought forward. The first flag I saw there in a small tucked away village made me gasp. I see any rainbow anywhere, in the sky or as an emblem in a corner store, I call out, oh there you are. Just like Rumi calling to his Beloved, "I see you and you see me."

Letting It Go

I see these boxes on porches around the neighborhood that are for recycling things that won't get recycled someplace else. I do my part and work my anxiety, anger, grief, despair. The daily work of sweeping the floor.

Changing It Up

My commitment is to have my doubt
and greed and fear liberated. I want
to give them to the earth
transformed. If part of the fuel in this
alchemical process is the dross,
I have more than I need to keep
the fire lit through the night.

Requirements To Meet You

First of all we truly have to long for the meeting just like the jokes about changing a light bulb and it really wanting to change. Next we have to feel our own suffering in order to have a clue about what it is like for somebody else. This is the hard part, the really hard part. Then there is the need to live like we believe it: everything, everything is connected.

Compassion Plus One Makes A Full Circle

This is simple math. We feel care for the undergoing we are experiencing and send compassion to self and one other person we know or don't know. We have flat out doubled the compassion in that moment. One plus one makes the world go round.

Mercy Me

Laments are being sung. The planet is burning. Littered cars line the road. Flooding takes over. We are coming clean. This is the only territory the phoenix knows. Shall we catch a ride?

Air Awareness

Tibetan mythology believes awakened women accomplished in meditation practice can fly. I tell this story to the young girl who has had years of dreaming of falling hollow in space, falling through, suspended, that she is in training to be a sky dancer flying with colorful banners, sensuous, belonging to the air.

The Goddess Watches Over

Always. In NW there is the legend, of Tsagaglala or "She Who Watches." Off of the Colombia River there is a petroglyph of this being with eyes of radiating circles. The predictions of our time are terrifying and here we are with the goddess calling us to bold love in this great turning.

Flow and Flux

This is my phrase for my neurological storms. I work hard to remember these words because they locate me in time when I am in the midst. I remember when I am "on the ground" this too will change. It seems like collectively we are perilously close to being on the ground. The nervous system of the world is doing a crazy buzzing. May this electric buzz call us awake. The miracle is changing the buzz to humming heard round the world. We sing our songs and the world changes its tune.

BLESSINGS

I don't know what to do with a word that I over use and other people do too. It is embarrassing. Still I use it most every day. What I can say is that I mean it: may you have joy and ease in your life. May I. Those wishes don't go away.

The Fourth Turning

Traditionally there is childhood,
adult householder, and being an elder.
Me, I am in the fourth turning. We can
choose a fourth turning at any point
in our life, although when it is taken it
is usually lined up with open space,
open time, tender heart. In the fourth
turning, we turn toward spirit. I run
to you. My heart is breaking open.
Desire is in every cell.

Character Structure

Odd phrase isn't it? It is part of my previous life of sitting with people, talking together, working to understand the psyche with all its twists and turns. It is what holds us together and gives us that particular signature that becomes a resonant identity. Now I am deconstructing what I carefully constructed. It is thrilling. Openness and forgiveness and faith keep the deconstruction going.

Present In My Heart

I like to do prayers a couple of times throughout the day and wanted a phrase to remind me. Traveling in Egypt several years ago I made use of the calls to prayer five times a day. I would pause and do my prayers with this phrase folding in with all the calls to prayer everywhere "present in my heart."

Prism

A line from a song "We are diamonds in the sun everyone of us." We are like the lotus which emerges from mud and we are like diamonds that come from depths and reveal themselves in an iridescent glimmer. In Buddhism the lotus is a frequently used metaphor of awakening. It is all there: the murky depths and the bright rising of mindfulness and kindness.

Meiji Shrine

A most holy Shinto shrine in the middle
of Tokyo. Like sacred temples all over,
people write and leave prayers.
Know that there are prayers for you
wishing you well being and
peace. There are prayers for you in
every language.

Bring Your Bathing Suit Or Not, Just Come Swimming

Your separateness sees my
separateness. We are messed up.
I have given up believing in
my separateness a while ago
but it still thinks it runs the show.
It can think whatever it wants.
I am swimming in the ocean.

Practices For The Time

Let's talk about technology. It is not a conversation I usually initiate but here we are. Let's talk about the technology of awareness. Let's say it is the highest order. Let's say it all begins with being conscious. This is how we traverse mind and spirit. I cultivate heart connection and awareness. I come to the Goddess. I come to the Beloved. May the blessings of the holy ones be with us as we walk the path of this time.

"Magic Is In The Air"

When someone says that you know the potential for sly pleasure is near. I call on magic most every day and say hey come play with me. Magic and I go back a long time. I tell magic if they want a good word put in, I would be glad to sing their praises. I know I can't carry a tune. That's okay. Mirth is in the air. Can you catch it?

Humor From The Void

Keeps on coming.

Cooked

I have been in the alchemical
cauldron a long time. So long
in fact I can't remember when
I wasn't. A number of times I have
emphatically declared "Enough!"
The fire is on. I am ash that transforms
to dream. My dream is of music and
dance and connection and you.

A Jerk Sometimes

The reasons for being a jerk sometimes are variations of feeling edgy disconnected in my being. Forgive me. I work two lines: my anxious, everyday self, and my spirit self. One is not more noble than the other.

I Am Here

I was given your riches and didn't give a nod. I gave a small nod yes but I was restrained. My regret. Let me return. Let me rest in your dazzling light.

Holy Work

Everyday it is the same holy task.
Today I met it. I saw a flock of
small birds fly past the hemlocks
in my neighbor's yard. Joy pure
for a moment.

THE DISTANCE OF LOVE

I am loved and
I love to be sure.
We work it to be sure.
It is an arduous road at times.
Love is bandied about
as the be all.
What I know is
this is my path
the distance
the length
I want to walk.

L'Amour

We were at a
phantasmagorical circus event
and standing near the emcee
at one of the performance circles.
It was early
the show hadn't begun.
My partner had arms around me
and we were gently swaying
and the emcee cries out "L'Amour"
on the microphone.
We were the spotlight.
We do sway with each other.
Who do you sway with?

The Antidote To Ego Investment

I don't believe my thoughts anymore.
I have intercepted them countless time.
They are silly and redundant.
My heart knows what is what.
I use to chase joy. Less so now.
I give over and make room for gratitude.
It leaves me empty and whole.

Speed Of Cherry Petals Falling Down

We seem to collectively be
in an imploding revolution of chaos.
Structures are coming down.
We are deconstructing.
We have done it before.
Part of the deal.
Cherry blossoms are
part of the deal as well.

The Fool and The Dog Walking Down The Road

I know what I look like
in my mind's eye.
Two beings walking
in the world, grinning,
happy to be between heaven
and earth.
Love dogs both of us.

A Different Part of the Brain

My life has been good and
it has been hard. I did
the worldly deeds that
the time called for with family,
work, play. I attended
to what was there and
had vision. Now I am in
different territory.
I listen to music for hours
each day. I walk. I dance.
I call out to you.

My Heart Is Met

Crazy in love meeting you
and you
meeting me.
I need to be
near you
and you say
you are
everywhere.
I have heard
that before.
Help me out here.
I lift the veil and see
numinous landscape
here and now, day and night,
and know myself going towards.

Gritty Today

I have cycles of physical distress.
It is part of my path.
I pay more loving attention
and that helps.
I give over.
I am limp.
I yield to what I cannot avoid.
This relinquishment is my offering.

My Dance Teacher

is doing a new series
"Next Steps."
The class is an hour and half.
It is taped and a copy
sent to all the dancers
for the next six weeks.
This is a teacher who
20 years ago had
t shirts made up with the note
"Dance Ugly and Drool."
You can't beat that.

Go Figure

The world is the Beloved and
we are all holy ones.

Headline From Newspaper Stand On The Corner

"The World Holds Us in
Iridescent Luminosity and
Peace and Amazing Grace."
This is the news from the world.

Aspirations

Skin and bones. Dropping importance. Dropping density. Dropping heaviness. Dropping opinions. Dropping the dross. I get to be that bleached bone on the shore, light streaming out in all directions.

Blue Sky Everywhere

Have you looked up recently? I just did and there is blue sky. The marker is though is there blue sky in my mind. It is one of my favorite metaphors: blue sky as the picture of the awakened heart mind. I look up and see blue sky peeking through the overcast sky of my mind. Feeling the presence of the blue sky expand. I'll take it.

This Culture

we are in does not treasure the
joining of the erotic and spirit.
As far as I can tell, they call to each
other. The sensate body and the
loving spirit want to gaze at other
and then some. It seems to be about
finding the beloved and going the
course of love and over the moon.

Careful

All my life, well most of my life, I have been careful. This is not an accolade. It was a survival mechanism I honed well. Now I am just plain giving over. I have nothing left but this expanse of possibility.

What There Is To Work With

Bring it down through the body the
rain of blessings. It touches dreaming,
dreaming the body awash in love.
Radiance of a star shouting out.

Competition

My partner always "wins" around feeling gratitude. This being is a 12 Stepper. I know struggle and I work it. Regularly enough ending up with gratitude. He has schooled his work to a community process that shares gratitude with each other on a daily basis. How can I compete?

Boogie Man

Scary stories with lots of challenges
and confrontations are read to
children. The lessons often revolve
around being generous and caring
to the demon who threatens you.
I get it now that fairy tales are what
they are to help us remember how
to find the path decades later when
we are in trouble. My boogie man
is a deeply familiar companion.
We sit by the side of the road chatting.

Flying Colors

Happiness and joy on a splendid day. I want resonance of this in my nervous system. I want a stable state with this. I want to be fully present to this good day in my heart and in my life.

All Right
It Is All Right

I don't know how to roller blade
but I believe I know how it feels.
This exhilaration of making all those
fun glides along the pavement and
the breeze mingled in. What I know
is how to walk in dreamtime. If I
catch it right, I am in this flow that
reminds me of the phrase "knee deep
in grace." Dreamtime walking in the
world is where you will find me.

Gold Watch

It was a playful deep gift given at a momentous time. It feels that since it is an instrument of time I could use it to get into mystic time.
May magic and mystery be with me. May magic and mystery be with you. May we open our hearts to awe. Between the watch and the mantras, I feel like I have a chance. When I make it in I will leave the door ajar. Let's walk together and find out what this is all about.

No Glamorizing Here

Shamans accept the brutality of their lives. They work understanding, power, wisdom from the broken open place. They say it is all there in the broken open place.

Baraqah

The Sufi term for divine blessing is something I negotiate everyday. It is such hard work and good fortune to be in heart connection with that which is open and beautiful and includes everything. It is the classic task for the seeker of getting out of their own way. The next formidable obstacle is how to give return. If you see someone with a friendly smile, who you don't know, waving at you from across the street it could be me sending greetings.

Ode to the Fool

The image for me of the fool is from the Tarot with the fool walking hill and dale. The ease of her heart is palpable. I walk just like the fool and on a good day I have wonder and the simple happiness of walking in the world. My happiness can be joined with my anxiety. I have tried walking it away, now I just send all my love to that old fear place and say softly "It is okay. Everything is okay."

It Routinely Annoys Me

when someone tells me to "relax." Don't they know that is what I want: to let go, let down. I won't go as far to say surrender which is another annoying word. "Give over" works. It is everything I want.

Synapse Between Self And God

It is that spark we have seen in glorious paintings. I exclaim when I see it outside of myself. Inside for me it can be a flash of understanding where everything makes sense. A unified field where good wishes person to person is like swaying at a concert, thousands of lights, synapses blinking all one wave.

Singing Me Home

You know that pattern you see
sometimes in people of being slower,
less cognition, more heartfulness.
With my own circumstances I am there.
It is such a relief.

My Hardship Is Polished

I see my reflection in the mirror,
the reflection left from all the polishing.
The heaviness is lifted. The density
is less. The image wavers like a
live shot on a camera. Humming
I move through.

Taking It Down

Dance the undoing. That is what I am doing. In the dance I have the spiral down. My circle is not bad. Moving through the planes. Sure.
I have spent a lifetime filling myself up and now here I am taking it down one dance move at a time. Dancing the liberation. The revolution begins at home. Time to take it down and fly.

Sweet Nothings

Dark matter, unseen matter here.
Devotion here. Clear light here.
We are all here. Evoking the heart
of the universe. The bliss of emptiness.
The radiance of space. I whisper
all this to you.

The Gesture That Calls It

The world was quiet in the beginning of the pandemic. I have coffee on the porch early morning and I can hear distant freeways in their quiet roar. It was quiet. Just plan quiet. Now on to regular days. Sometimes it feels simple like hands on the heart. Sometimes it doesn't. Either case hands on the heart covers it all.

A Nod

Sign seen in a convenience store: "Be kind everyone is fighting a great battle." Just today in the drug store the clerk said as I entered "Hello Sugar." I took it right in and gave a nod back.

Thich Nhat Hanh

I got through years of dense challenge with the "half smile" he talked about. It was my practice everyday. To the earth, to my spirit, I meet you here. This is my willingness.

Hanuman

I feel giddy imagining Hanuman's great devotion to Rama. I knew early on that devotion was the spirit fast track yet I chose cultivation of awareness and mindfulness as a primary path. Awareness is purification it just is taking longer than I expected.

The Speed Of Our Time

The raga teaches speed. Yet as I listen I let down. Maybe the speed is already there and the raga mirrors that wisdom. In any case, I jump into the sound. I float in sound waves all sense of speed gone.

A Call

One of my neurological symptoms
is feeling on the edge of my skin.
Sometimes I can think of other people
who feel similar and send compassion
to us, sometimes I can't. I miss you
there. I know you are there somewhere.
Come to me on the edge of my skin.

No Grace Here

Or so I thought. Just by itself now
I have blips, images of previous times.
I am embarrassed, sometimes shame
is there, and over and over lack of
grace. No longer do I start from
those images. Come darling and
let me hold you. I hold you with such
peace and care.

Remake The World

My quickening is vulnerability. I do my work and the vulnerability is exposed. My defenses let down and openness fills in. As you know this is not a fun process. It is what I choose in order to see you everywhere

Such A Simple Statement

Be present with what is. It is
formidable being with what is,
it takes everything. Not that I
get there for long. The difficulty
is not paying attention, the alternative,
is not much better. It can cause all
manner of trouble. This moment
acceptance. No promises for the next.

A Mystic Rant

Gaia the goddess bodhisattva is
all around. Right here, right now.
We are held with a jewel like luminosity.
We are held in love and kindness
every moment. The rant is really a
chant deep in the planet that we
are beginning to hear. Calling out.
We are held in the deepest care.

This Too

The bell tolling is the bell of awakening. Day or night, well or dying, the bell says come on home. Home for me is accepting the hardship of my life, inhabiting the good, and being a work in progress. I am particularly weary of the last one. The light from being a work in progress flickers like a naked bulb from the ceiling.

Job Description For A Shaman

It is to be able to see, to travel, and to travel back. Seeing light and dark, seeing into the 10 directions, seeing what is missing, seeing what went wrong. Traveling is across time to the past and to the future, seeing into the heart of those that come for help. Call and response with the elements and something changes.

COLLECTING

I admit it: I am a collector. I collect books, art, plants for the garden, clothes. It has been a pleasure.
Now I am turning around that axis inside and singing once again.
This singing is soft, almost a whisper saying I am ready for what is next.

UNBOUNDED

Revelatory. Ecstatic. Vast. The heart that has no bounds. Bigger than we can imagine.

Where To Go For A Night Swim

It is that pond down the road that
you drive by on the way to town.
The night sky illuminated in the pond.
Splashing around in the galaxy.

Sugar

Street people will sometimes hail me with "Sugar." I am not offended. On the contrary, I am impressed that there is such affection for someone they don't even know. I send them my warm regard.

You and Me Both

This elderly Indian woman and I sat next to each other on a long flight. We didn't have a common language yet we shared food and an unspoken knowing with each other. We both could feel the gift of this quiet nestling in with each other. Once off the plane, I had to run to make my next flight. I turned around for a moment and there she was in the crowd. I waved and she waved back.

A Line Of Light

The horizon is stunning. Over and over again, there is this line of light at the intervals of the day and night. It is where I go to remember where I came from.

Following The Arc Of The Land

In some ways, I have been a straight arrow. Not that those days are over but I have to tell you I cut a mean curve. It takes me around the world. I am that person who stops in their tracks in front of you pointing exclaiming about the beauty all around.

All Of One Piece

Happy joy. To be connected to heart, body, you.

Reckoning

Don't know how my heart will weigh in at death against a feather of the Egyptian goddess Maat. Access to the higher regions is given if one's heart weighs less than the feather. What I do know is that after struggle I am lighter. I get lighter each day.

Grace Takes Over

There was a festive gathering planned. Preparations and prayers for all manner of good in place. Then it happened: connection, good cheer, celebration. Grace can happen any old time of course. We do everything we do and then something else carries us.

Darling I Am Here

I say this to the air, to myself on a hard day, to my partner on a hard day. It is such comfort. I know various things. Perhaps this is one of the most important understandings: showing up expressive and real.

Wheelhouse Of Time

I have had an anxious relationship to time. The usual stuff: everything from not enough time to the tedium of it all. My reveal after decades of trying to get this is time becomes potentially spacious if I am securely in my body. You know connected to awareness and breath and heart.

LONELY

Not much but it still happens.
Whew it can carry a sting. I bless
my forlornness. I bless my
disconnection. With this feeling
flowing into openness like a tributary
into a river love and care to every cell.

The Wicked Witch Is Dead

A friend took me out. Did well. On my feet I wondered "What do I do?" I got some traction when I realized it is an inside job. I get to work with these instructions: disarm the dynamic where I participate in any way with being taken out. Working on it.

Spirit Time

I sit on the stoops letting the spring
sun warm me. My dog is here too.
We soak up the radiance of it all. The
light changes but the radiance doesn't.

The Work Of Coming Home

The holy is always near. See the holy everywhere. Know the holy. I do mostly. I return to awareness and compassion and call it good. Holy days and nights are made of this: returning over and over again saying "Here I am."

Receiving

grace. I polish my bones, say my
prayers, blow kisses to the universe,
or in other words get all aligned, and
can still have trouble receiving the
juicy good. I get busy or distracted.
Undergoing nips at my heels.
Sometimes I am just a mess, sometimes
I am ashes from the fire of change,
sometimes receiving is easy.
Moment to moment a discovery.

What Does Shame Have To Do With It

Everything. A couple of seconds of shame and we are out of the room. We may have left but the shame didn't. It is still boomeranging in the psyche looking for a place to land. Hands on the heart: I see you, I am sorry we are hurting. This is how we take care returning to the heart over and over. Finding peace in the midst.

Presence Is A Good Thing

It took some convincing for me. Seeing the overlap with charisma is uncomfortable. I preferred to keep it all quiet, on the down low. Proclaiming or hiding are part of the same protest. Either way we are far from presence, that big loving acceptance of self that kisses the sky.

Tipping The Scales

I know how. I truly do. Prayer is the vehicle. Calling to the numinous to help. I am not suggesting we put in a request and wait for mystery to stock the order. It has taken me a while to appreciate that is not the way it works. Just recently I said a prayer for my neighbor who is in the hospital. What I can tell you with certainly is that she is held in love and mystery. Don't know more than that.

LUSHNESS

A grey moist autumn afternoon
walking in my neighborhood park.
For some reason the lampposts were
on and there was a golden hue
mixed with the yellow gold resonance
of color from the trees. Walking in the
dream is how I want to live my life.

Use What You Have

Cooks can challenge each other with that directive: use what you have. So can science projects. Rainmakers do the same. Rainmakers in the traditional sense of restoring harmony to a land. They have their internal being place of peace and bring it with them wherever they go.

Initiatory Fees

A mythic thing this place of initiatory rite of passage in order to benefit the village. The fee is high. It takes dedication to withstand the trials and enormous devotion to the welfare of others. This is a whale rider. Or it could be an eagle rider. Or it could be a coyote rider. We take care of others and the animals witness.

In The Mix

I have experienced cycles of difficulty in my life. I could give you particulars but you know the story. I change it up. I feel more. I grieve when it is there. This isn't about saying oh more acceptance of these places and the ache will go away. Not necessarily saying that. I am saying blow a kiss to this tenderness and keep walking.

Mending The Time

What a crossroads this is: old wounding, lots of history on one corner and the corner across from it a deep well with clear water. The other corner is a flag post with an iridescent banner undulating in the breeze. The fourth corner is our collective culture. It is dense, technical energy with rural overtones. Churning turmoil that hasn't decided where it is going.
I am familiar with each path. I am traveling east building cairns along the way to help me find my bearings in this mythic time.

Using Everything In Order To Write

Rather it is using everything to live well. Every thoughtful kind glorious thing that we have experienced. There is more you say. Sure and for all the hurt and violence it is ours to chew it up until it is digestible. There is much to get to and I am right where I am meant to be.

Less Of Me

Externally I am about the same.
Interiorly I feel mighty thin.
This may be what it looks like in
this fourth turning the turning toward
spirit. Less of me until I rise free
in your love.

Know Your Deep Goodness

Know your deep goodness.
It is the most truthful thing about you.
It is calling your name.

Openness Being Known

I start with my chest wide and
strong, then I check in with mind
and awareness, from there to heart
expression. It's working. With a
little attending I am making it through
the day openness being known.
Way more interesting.

Over The Moon

Sensuality revealed with bliss and great joy.

Mystical Relational Core

I know that is a mouthful. What I like about the phrase is that it is all there: the bliss of Great Mother, the relationship that interacts with it all, and the knowing deep inside. I aim for the horizon. Light sparkling like faceted jewels. Unified.

The Sacred Void and Dream Dance

I work on this dance everyday. It is my testimonial of belonging. I serve you here with my gliding, my playful devotion, my turning on the greater axis. It is also the reckoning and at some point will be my last dance witnessed by spirit. May you grin with delight at this offering.

Say What

I tend to be soft spoken. Shy too.
On this spirit road I turn over to you.
A thousand times. Rejoicing.

No New News

Flawed. Can't seem to get away from it. Seems like just part of what is there. The good news is this flawed place is getting a bit blurry and folding in with the larger design.

Back Heart

It sings to us doesn't it? It seems to be a different tune for every person. A cacophony of sound if we put it all together. Mine is my knowing, that is, my back heart tells me what is true. I trust the cacophony to let the chaos in and lead me to what is worthy and wise.

THE VEIL IS THIN TODAY

Numerous people are saying that.
The Day of the Dead is upon us.
Marigolds and altars and sugar treats.
A good picnic with remembrances
and offerings. In the midst of the
festivities we listen deeply.

Dropping Prayers

Rumi talked about doing that as he walked. I imagine snow flakes as your prayers. I imagine plum blossoms flying down as your prayers. I imagine rose petals on the ground as your prayers. I imagine fall leaves swirling down as your prayers. Beauty and prayers giving to us across time.

Beginner's Mind

Wondering how beginner's mind plays out with loving someone deeply, seeing them and being seen. I have been in a beloved relationship for decades. We work it well. Duress schools us. Still. There is happiness and stretches of serious work. We have the experience it takes for beginner's mind and sometimes the marvel.

A Completion Of The Circle With These Four

These diamond jewels are available on a daily basis. We call them out and are changed. Necessary is compassion for self. Kindness in some form everyday. Gratitude as the be all and end all. Openness as a stance for making the best of this life. Here it is compassion, kindness, gratitude, openness. The holy grail of a life lived well.

Prayers Heard Around The World

Your prayer. My prayer. May we all be safe and our hearts at ease. This prayer of good will went out to everyone. Prayers just work like that.

Open Floor Practice

Inquiry into the mind with sitting meditation and inquiry into embodiment on the open dance floor. The structure of joy.

Affection Love Gratitude

The park I walk everyday is several hundred acres of trails with some gain and stretch out places. Something changes inside me walking this as a practice. Sensual connection with this dreamtime wholeness unties the knots of my heart. Day after day.

People Do Fly

A title of a painting at the Detroit Art Institute that is an echo in my psyche. Tibetan sky dancers fly why can't I? This ability to fly is part of the soul's DNA. Sky dancers are famous for their sensual embodiment and enlightened presence. School me in being awakened and loving. School me in lucidity and wisdom. School me. I am here.

The Lineage Of Devotion

Hanuman devoted to Ram. Utterly. This amazing monkey was pure in devotion. I am part of this lineage. I have led a disciplined life now I am undone with devotion. Let us call out. Let us purify our hearts. Let us sing chants that have been handed down in this lineage for thousands of years. Let us come together in praise of all that is holy.

Blue Hills

I know these hills from taking my son to the Eagle Cap Wilderness area. It is a dry spacious land. If there are no fires the air is clean. Wide open and peaceful. I travel through this land glad to be alive.

Movement Of Mind

Many days it can be breezy in the mind. Turbulence and agitation come and go. There is a prayer in the mystic cannon "All is well. Well being for all." Listening in and hearing the prayers just carrying on. Comfort in this mystic revolution of compassion. Prayers inside and prayers outside colliding calling our hearts awake.

The Chevron

I have deciphered its meaning: it is an arrow pointing to God. What a handy signpost. We all get lost and forlorn at times and like signposts in a fairytale the chevron gives us bearings. It reminds us when we have veered off course and says "Here, this way is filled with wisdom and goodness." The path is worn and well cared for.

Flood Plains

I am there now. It is nourishing to all of me. Devotion renewing the day.

Try It Out

A heart of love generates rainbow iridescence, a field of boundless compassion. May there be well being and happiness for all. May there be peace and safety for all. Far reaching ongoing good wishes. No holding back.

Dedicating Merit

This is a Buddhist practice to give back the blessing of our good deeds. Merit is like gold coins of the spirit. Giving it away is a straightforward way to share the wealth with a net of interconnectivity. Generosity in motion over the long haul.

It Is All There

I feel my transgressions, my little
shames, my closed down places.
It is all there. I make room to feel it.
The more I make room the more
I am okay. Allowing air to touch
my skin and heal my insides.

Home Ground

Working with openness. Finding it and losing it. I return in my heart to the blue sky expanse, to the clear light of the heart, to reverence. Dancing this ground.

For Somebody Else

Even for people I dislike I send
compassion. For myself I forget.
Not today. I remember you. I remember
others. I remember to come back
to me like a whisper wanting more.

Best Friend

My best friend lives in Italy. We send each other photos and postcards of art around us. Just today he said to me "It, of course, reminded me of you, your confidence in exploring what lies ahead, unknown but welcomed." Sweetheart right. May your friend speak to you in a language your heart understands and everything will be all right.

My Heart Is Available

Worked all my life for this and here
I am. Sitting on the cushion throughout
my adult years. What good fortune.
Steady practice bringing me to
my heart.

Swap Meet

I have good qualities. You have good
qualities. I don't know about you but
I have an abundance of some
qualities and really little of others.
Let's exchange. Like my dance teacher
would instruct if you like a move
of another dancer take it on, try it out.
Making whole cloth as we can.

Pivot Point

    The body records memories.
    The heart records memories.
    In the moving through, in the creating,
    we see the richness of what is there.
    Memories blessed.
    A new life begins.

Dreamtime and The Path With Heart

This is my distillation of what is real. It is all that I know. Rather all that I know on good days. The translation reads fluid reality infused with seeing and magic and faith.

Smooth Sneakers

This is about the soles which is like my brain. There is not quite enough texture to get traction sometimes. Quite remarkable. Maybe a link to you is understanding physical struggle and knowing the need to walk to God because that is all there is. I know you get it.

A Directive To My DNA

I told my son he could inherit my admirable qualities but not the difficult frustrating ones. I am telling my DNA the same thing. Let's cut the dross right from the start. It gives me a chance.

Mystic Warrior

Longing, love, knowing and an incredible discipline. The discipline equals the task: purification of being unconscious in a trance dull overwhelmed. Freedom is an aware loving heart. The work endures across time.

Sumptuous Joy Now And Then

I do the spiritual rituals of purification.
And yet joy flat out joy seems to be
just around the next corner. What's
with that? I protest. What I have is
appreciation of my gratitude
returning to this like a compass
in the woods
the resonant light carrying the day.

Nervous System As The Double

If my nervous system is my doppelgänger I am in trouble. A rogue nervous system with random firings and misdirection. Okay. It just means it is all there. Working chaos. Working acceptance. It is all there.

Mystic Lover Of The World

The path with heart has such radiance.
We walk this path and the world is
revealed like lovers discovering the
mystery of the night
luminosity giving over.

Somewhere Over the Rainbow

Working it to make the leap .
Working it to lighten the load.
All my carefully chosen concepts give
ballast. So much weight it is hard
to get off the ground. Chop chop
I want to fly.

Sureness Of
An Arrow

You may not know this about me
but I am good at predicting the gold
winners in individual Olympic events.
There is that sheen of excitement a
person carries that says they can do
what they set out for and then some.
Just watch. The talent and training
entrained. The beauty outrageous.
The intrinsic grace made visible.
Rightful like none other.

Arrow Through The Void

My intent carries me. Across my own divides. To you dear friend. For all of us whose skin and spirit got separated along the way. For all my relations. May God's love be with us. Here we are open hearted mystical lovers of the divine. It is everyday life. It is the arrow finding its course.

Casting Lines to the Future

Wishes prayers ribbons the tree is
beautiful. Wishes prayers ribbons
the fence is beautiful. Wishes prayers
ribbons the holy wall is beautiful.
Wishes prayers ribbons the
neighborhood altar is beautiful.
All around the world colorful strips
of cloth blowing in the wind.
With these diamond jewels we
create the world.

Body Breathing Moves With Time

Finding breathing noting breath.
I breathe I move I pray. Time keeps
up with me and me with time.
I am present and resourced.

What We Have Come To

Bluebirds sing. Sunday promenade
around the grove of trees at the
summit of the park. Archetypal really.
All manner of beings kids dogs.
Returning to simple pleasure.
Returning to what we know in
our bones brings peace.

Riffing

A jazz phrase becomes more lyrical.
A gesture becomes more outrageous.
A prayer becomes more about touching
the Milky Way. Freedom no constraint
connected in the keenest way to
others. We lean in to each other
to understand the collective path.
We pray for great harmony and
hear an echo in the valley.

Shaping The Day

The room in Hanoi we stayed in
when visiting was a corner room with
windows looking out to the busy street
below. It was cut up oddly with
different lengths walls. I liked it
immediately. There was a small desk
looking out one of the windows.
I had a flash of another time being
a writer in this intriguing city.
Memory all around.

Tiny Stings And Misunderstandings

I am feeling it. I know I give it out as well. What a tangle. This seems to call not for a tougher skin rather a heap more compassion for all the folly we partake in. Back to the phrase "We are all idiots. Be kind."

Being A Prayer Wheel In The World

Two hands on the heart "May we all be free and happy." Here with this wish of loving kindness we have touched with our prayer every sentient being. Two hands on the heart covers a distance. It is a distance we can walk everyday. Then when you meet a person any person you know you have already sent blessings.

Way Complicated

Complex systems theory or something like that. Feeling this knowing about my heart connected to your heart. We can get messed up as we sort it all out. Love is part of that theory. Bringing it home and belonging. Laughing together most every day. We find our way.

Heart Presence

Dreamtime is the world. We witness and say prayers "May God's love be with you" and go on.

Eyes At The Horizon

That way we can include the earth and the sky in one glance remaking our perception. Here we live big enough with ease.

Once Again

Forgetting to send compassion
to self when in the midst. Sheepishly
I acknowledge that it has happened
before. This is part of the lifeline to
spirit. I come to you whatever my
circumstances. So I say. This time
I mean it.

Jai Ma

Oh mother. Help me. Help us all. Let our offering be seeing the sweet truth, talent, sorrow of others. An offering that has unending vision.

Writing Code For My Spirit

Vibrant resonant joy awe mystery reverence play. May there be grace in doing my work and going the distance. Just this.

Field Relationship

"The field is the only reality." Einstein was such a field mystic. Me too. It is how I understand working chance and luminosity and connection. I feel it as the space that holds me. I feel it as conversation and mutuality. I feel it as well being in my skin.

Down Come The Walls

There are historical examples of
course. Let's talk personal revolutions
of awakening that move the earth.
Broken open smashed to smithereens.
A Zen koan that recognizes itself.

Noticing What Comes From Mind

Any urban context and I can find
representations of the goddess.
Musing where will I see the goddess
today? Mind like a mirror. I know
she is near. I find her and she finds me.
It is like a child's game of hide and seek
being found is the happiest thing ever.

Mystic Time

Field is the presence of all that
is holy. Watch out for benevolence,
magic, sometimes heaps of work
to get to what is real and true.
Held truly. Safe and well. Happy
and connected. Basking in the
winter sun my heart takes this right in.

Mind

or openness brightness awareness.
I guess it is easier to just say "mind"
but you don't want to leave
anything out.

Bless Your Heart

An old phrase that has many
meanings. It speaks of the
field of the heart. It speaks
of range and nuance.
May this acknowledgement
fly from person to person,
community to community.
May it give us just what we need.

Tundra Swans Flying

Swans have been too elegant for me. Their perfection is a bit much. In any case I have changed my view about swans by seeing them fly in small groups. Whew the most beautiful effortless flight through light and air. Sandhill cranes on the ground gathering. Kestrel on a post. Gratitude.

Mindstream

Mindstream and river stream are they different? Mindstream carrying all our thoughts and experiences. Training the mind they are seen as ephemeral and gossamer. River movement moving through time carrying our faith our peace and well being. River running beauty like none other. Walking through the world, walking through the mindstream there is care and goodness and everything else.

Daily Practice

Feeling the light of the world
in my heart.

Spirit Talent

I have only recently realized mine.
Almost startling to see how my
perseverance has been really faith.
I am steady and disciplined. Other
things too but steadfastly working
the path. My head has been bent
to the task. I look up and I can see
I am traveling the distance to see you
my faith knowing the course.

HEY

Like everybody I have my regular self. Okay. Fine. Yet it seems such a long crossing to get to you from there.
I listen to music for hours, I walk and walk, there is a moment more of continuity with my practice yet my heart has that everyday ache. I am going to go dive into my music. Catch you later.

Remembering To Remember

Seriously I need to write myself
a note "remember the holy goddess."
What kind of mind do I have?
I believe a fairly regular one. If it is
about remembering to write notes
I have it covered. If it is about
sustaining spirit attention in order
to find devotional bliss that is the path.
I return over and over again.
That is my path.

Washed Through With Light

Openness all around healed and whole this moment. Iridescence all around healed and whole this moment. The long course of love begins here.

Relational Field

I know solitary sure for periods
of my life. More and more what
I feel is how you dear field meet me.
No me no you just heart presence.

Pilgrim Heart Devotion

Wherever I go. This is the pilgrimage.

Dharma Warrior

Sometimes scared and sacred seem like the front and back of who we are with all that goodness and complexity intertwined. The fearlessness it takes for us to be lit from the inside. The path holding the wisdom we need.

Changing Paradigms

One of the quickest ways to do that in this cognitive dominant culture is to go to the experience of the body. The attention to sense sensation the embodiment brings us round. We reorient. We know what's what. Body and heart mind needing each other. Our culture needing us whole.

Shirofugen Cherry As Taoist Elder

This shirofugen has been through it weathering all kinds of damage. Now it is a small delicate yet sturdy tree. It helps that so much has been chopped off. Only what is needed to survive is left. Grace evident in the frail body branching. The mantra "only this now" comes to mind.

Metadata

It is all dreamtime that tuned
responsive back and forth
that being time. That place where
the field is a friend and the world
is a benefactor. I rely on the give
and take that unfolds in the waking
dream showing me a map of true self,
the belonging and going towards
the nervous system trained in light.

Decency and Hard Times

We all have those old hard times yeh we do. May we develop our good hearts along the way. May we give thanks to the interconnectivity that holds us with such decency and care. May we find the intersection with magic wherever we are. This is a definition of grace: doing one's work with the help of others and going the distance.

Faceted Jewels Everyone Of Us

Tibetan Buddhism talks about
the rainbow as the luminous body
of the diety or holy person.
Like auras of radiant light.
We do our part by cultivating heart
wisdom strengthening loving presence.
After basic needs the need to be
beloved is first. In this luminous
relational world we call other
"beloved" and are called in return
"beloved."

Routine and Revelation

The world is outrageously sensuous. It is there wherever a person looks. Day after day the world meeting our gaze.

Lay It Down

Crusty patterns that I have carried
a long time is what I want to lay down.
Burrowed in to be sure and worked it
repeatedly. Just the way it is with
those tap roots that go to center of
the earth. Feels like that anyway.
Done with the descent on this one.
The tap root is coming out entirely
this time. Mark my words.

The Edge Of The World

The city I live in is coming back from several years of disruption and upheaval. Restaurant lights. The rest of the block boarded up and tagged. Collective revolution on going justice issues predominantly. We are in it. For a stretch. The necessity of change. The ground is shifting. Spirit practice joining with the times understanding dissolution.

Weave Of Wholeness

Breathing the world inside me. Breathing the world outside me. In process with continuity of awareness. In process with the rough and tumble. In process with prayer. For a moment all of one piece.

Riff Raff

We are out there to be sure
on the streets. We are dissolute.
Just take me for an example I don't
look like riff raff but you never know.
That depth is in me. You bet. I carry it
with me. Bless us all.

Lines Of Memory

We all inherit this spiral of memory.
I have been sorting through this tangle looking at places where I carry "badness." To be sure it is present. Kind of like the making of fine perfume and using a foul scent as part of the synergy. It is there and collaborates with the other oils. Me too.

Seed Intents

I created intent around devotion and practice in my twenties. Decades later here I am finding joy with the aspirations I named then. It feels amazing to cross through time the prayers leading the way.

I Walk Gratitude

Needing an expression for all
this feeling for you. Needing wanting
all the longing to be received by you.
I found my way. I walk I send you
praise I give gratitude to the sky
and the earth. I trust all is well.
This is my offering.

A Means To Keep Close

Combining breathing awareness with attention to the heart center. I say the words to myself "compassion to all" as I exhale. Doing this as my devotion. Over and over.

The Sun and The Moon

Perhaps the sun how we shine
is the front heart. Perhaps the moon
how we feel is the back heart.
Perhaps the sun is compassion to all.
Perhaps the moon is walking
gratitude being gratitude. The sun
and the moon giving instruction
and blessings.

The Light Walking On Grey Mornings

Almost my favorite. My practice is to walk everyday. I have been doing this for years and make it most every day. Got to say the saturation of essence is vivid when there are no shadows. Looking at form and line without any distractions. Resplendent really.

FRACTURED YOU BET

If we are lucky we heal along the way.
Some of us get the chance. I don't
know if the fractured goes away,
It can become Indra's Net with its
understanding of interconnectivity.
It can become the sun catching the
light of a stone. It can become
anything. What do you imagine?
A sunflower being fractals the
healed version of fractured.

The World Lit From Within

Awareness purifies. Remember
the hologram of awareness looks
like the night sky from a mountain top.
The awareness lighting the world
from the inside.

"Harmonize Darling"

Murmuring to myself when I am in the midst. Softly present with this dreamtime self. Remembering acceptance. Looking out and seeing that the rain has stopped and blessings are flying down.

The Goodness That Is You

And you, and you, and you.

The Mystical Field

Saw the total solar eclipse 2017 from a small town baseball field. The field goes entirely dark and the birds stopping singing people next to us broadcasting Richard Strauss. Attending to awe and mystery.

The Ministry That Calls To Us Each

Tending the body. The practice of being in the body touching feeling listening moving. Tending the nervous system that impartial recorder of time. I do both. We all do one way or another.
Today changing my scared separate body into a magic body of love.
The nervous system giving a thumbs up much better choice.

A Thing Of Beauty

Today some kids in a preschool group were climbing up a significant hill and then rolling down. A little bumpy and fun. This one kid was different with their long continuous gliding roll to the bottom of the hill. The super power of trust and pleasure combined.

Train The Heart Like A Warrior

Love everyone. It is daunting devotion
to love everyone. I understand truly.
I negotiate with myself about what to
bring to the world. Clear
response: see from the heart and
let care flow to prayer.
Here the world is seen through
love all around.

Like A Wave

New understanding that moments of joy are intermixed with everything else that is going on in that moment that joy contains the previous moment as well as the next moment. Relief to feel this undulating continuum knowing that joy is a wave that contains the magnitude of the ocean and the discreteness of a poem.

Whole Cloth

I see it as Joseph's coat of many colors. This fine tapestry uses dreams to stitch the seams. We all have spent time in the well calling out. Joseph practiced flying and found the way out.

Immersed In Clear Light

Bliss moving through.

The Refrain

Give over because it is the annihilation.
Give over to keep walking on the
dusty road to the Beloved. I have
current nicks and old scars from
falling down. I feel lighter dancing this
ground, tumbleweed with internal light,
blowing in the wind. Here we are
finding harmony a shimmering of light
the ground and the sky meeting.

We are the light and the ground.
We are here dancing this ground.

We are the light and the ground.
We are here dancing this ground.

Rilke's Praise

In the stillness of the summer day,

white clouds make nests

in the mountains, the canoe drifts

gently awash in the current.

The lake spacious, witnessing

the gladness of work completed,

thresholds crossed in the deep,

the sun and the moon

blessing the tides that flow.

A Summary: A Long Poem

First Love Place Holder For Emptiness
Joining Power And Love Love Dog
Quickening And

Good Tidings Getting My Red Shoes
On Iridescence In The Field You And
Me A Broad Wing

Span Not Fixed Emergency Flashlight
Rainbow Flag Letting It Go Changing
It Up Requirements

To Meet You Compassion Plus One
Makes A Full Circle Mercy Me Air
Awareness The Goddess

Watches Over Flow And Flux Blessings
The Fourth Turning Character Structure
Present In My

Heart Prism Meiji Shrine Bring Your
Bathing Suit Or Not Just Come
Swimming Practices For

The Time "Magic Is In The Air"
Humor From The Void Cooked A Jerk
Sometimes I Am Present

Holy Word Work The Distance Of
Love L'Amour The Antidote To Ego
Investment Speed Of

Cherry Petals Falling Down The Fool
And The Dog Walking Down The Road
A Different Part Of

The Brain My Heart Is Met Gritty
Today My Dance Teacher Go Figure
Headline From

Newspaper Stand On The Corner
Aspirations Blue Sky Everywhere
This Culture Careful What

There Is To Work With Competition
Boogie Man Flying Colors All Right
It Is All Right Gold

Watch No Glamorizing Here Baraqah
Ode To The Fool It Routinely Annoys
Me Synapse

Between God And Self Singing Me
Home My Hardship Is Polished Taking
It Down Sweet

Nothings The Gesture That Calls It
A Nod Thich Nhat Hanh Hanuman
The Speed Of Our Time

A Call No Grace Here Remake
The World Such A Simple Statement
A Mystic Rant This Too

Job Description For A Shaman
Collecting Unbounded Where To Go
For A Night Swim Sugar

You And Me Both A Line Of Light
Following The Arc Of The Land All
Of One Piece Reckoning

Grace Takes Over Darling I Am Here
Wheelhouse Of Time Lonely
The Wicked Witch Is Dead

Spirit Time The Work Of Coming Home
Receiving What Does Shame Have
To Do With It

Presence Is A Good Thing Tipping
The Scales Lushness Use What You
Have Initiatory Fees In

The Mix Mending The Time Using
Everything In Order To Write Less
Of Me Know Your Deep

Goodness Openness Being Known
Over The Moon Mystical Relational
Core The Sacred Void

And Dream Dance Say What No
New News Back Heart The Veil Is Thin
Today Dropping

Prayers Beginner's Mind A Completion
Of The Circle With These Four Prayers
Heard Around

The World Open Floor Practice
Affection Love Gratitude People Do
Fly The Lineage Of

Devotion Blue Hills Movement Of
The Mind The Chevron Flood Plains
Try It Out Dedicating

Merit It Is All There Home Ground
For Somebody Else Best Friend
My Heart Is Available Swap

Meet Pivot Point Dreamtime And
The Path With Heart Smooth Sneakers
A Directive To My

DNA Mystic Warrior Sumptuous Joy
Now And Then Nervous System As
The Double Mystic

Lover Of The World Somewhere Over
The Rainbow Sureness Of An Arrow
Arrow Through The

Void Casting Lines To The Future Body
Breathing Moves With Time What
We Have Come To

Riffing Shaping The Day Tiny Stings
And Misunderstanding Being A Prayer
Wheel In The World

Way Complicated Heart Presence
Eyes At The Horizon Once Again
Jai Ma Writing Code For

My Spirit Field Relationship Down
Come The Walls Noticing What
Comes From Mind Mystic

Time Mind Bless Your Heart Tundra
Swans Flying Mindstream Daily
Practice Spirit Talent Hey

Remembering To Remember Washed
Through With Light Relational Field
Pilgrim Heart

Devotion Dharma Warrior Changing
Paradigms Shirofugen Cherry As
Taoist Elder Metadata

Decency And Hard Times Faceted
Jewels Everyone Of Us Routine And
Revelation Lay It Down

The Edge Of The World Weave Of
Wholeness Riff Raff Lines Of Memory
Seed Intents I Walk

Gratitude A Means To Keep Close
The Sun And The Moon The Light
Walking On Grey

Mornings Fractured You Bet The World
Lit From Within "Harmonize Darling"
The Goodness

That Is You The Mystical Field
The Ministry That Calls To Us Each
A Thing Of Beauty Train The

Heart Like A Warrior Like A Wave
Whole Cloth Immersed In Clear Light
The Refrain

www.ingramcontent.com/pod-product-compliance
Lightning Source LLC
Chambersburg PA
CBHW062243300426
44110CB00034B/1353